Finding Rest

A DEVOTIONAL

JENNIFER R. HECKER

Copyright © 2020 by Jennifer Hecker

All rights reserved. This book or any portion thereof may not be reproduced or used in any manner whatsoever without the express written permission of the publisher except for the use of brief quotations in a book review.

Printed in the United States of America
ISBN 978-0-578-75487-1

First Printing, 2020

Formatted by Sheenah Freitas of Paper Crane Books
papercranebooks.com

To my Husband Joeseph Hecker, whom I traveled across the United States with as he worked as a consultant to Utility Companies. Traveling with him gave me the incentive and time to write the devotionals and paint at my leisure.

To my son Joey Hecker who helped me connect with the digital world of the internet to get my worked edited and published.

His Eye is on the Sparrow

There is a popular song with lyrics that says, "His eye is on the sparrow /And I know He watches me."

God sees, He hears, and He knows. He is concerned about the smallest details of our lives.

He sees our struggles, our weakness, our fears.

He hears our prayers, our disappointment, and our cries for help.

He knows our DNA, our personality, our strong will, our passion for change, and the frustration of our situation.

Are not two sparrows sold for a copper coin? And not one of them falls to the ground apart from your Father's will. But the very hairs of your head are numbered. Do not fear therefore; you are of more value than many sparrows.

MATTHEW 10:29-31 (NKJV)

The physician Luke penned Jesus' words a little differently.

Are not five sparrows sold for two copper coins? And not one of them is forgotten before God. But the very hairs of your head are all numbered. Do not fear therefore; you are of more value than many sparrows.

LUKE 12:7 (NKJV)

Twice now the scripture is commanding us "do not fear." Jesus is speaking about unhealthy fears. The kind we entertain and carry with us that bring doubt and sometimes discouragement. Do not fear because Jesus loves you and values you more than many sparrows. The sparrow seems insignificant in the chain of life. We are not small and insignificant in the Father's eyes. We are His prized possession, He counts the very hairs on our head.

I Am God

"For you have trusted in your wickedness;

You have said 'No one sees me';

Your wisdom and your knowledge have warped you;

And you have said in your heart,

I *am* and *there is* no one else besides me."

ISAIAH 47:10 (NKJV)

How many nonbelievers do you know? Our institutions of higher learning have kicked God off their campuses: secular universities, public schools that are high schools, junior high schools, and elementary schools. Many public schools do not even acknowledge Christmas as a holiday. It is now called "winter break" all because of the "Christ" in Christmas.

> "Look to Me, and be saved,
> All you ends of the earth!
> For I *am* God, and *there is* no other.
> I have sworn by Myself;
> The word has gone out of My mouth *in* righteousness,
> And shall not return,
> That to Me every knee shall bow,
> Every tongue shall take an oath.
> He shall say
> 'Surely in the LORD I have righteousness and strength.
> To Him *men* shall come,
> And all shall be ashamed
> Who are incensed against Him.'"
>
> ISAIAH 45:22–24 (NKJV)

> I *am* God, and *there is* no other.
>
> ISAIAH 46:9 (NKJV)

He speaks His word. God is not silent. For generations He has told us who He is. He speaks in righteousness. He speaks all that is right and true.

He spoke a word and created us. Someday every knee will bow and acknowledge Him. Those who did not acknowledge Him will be ashamed that they did not give Him glory.

Paul tells us in Romans, "For since the creation of the world His invisible *attributes* are clearly seen, being understood by the things that are made, *even* His eternal power and Godhead, so that they are without excuse, because, although they knew God, they did not glorify *Him* as God, nor were thankful, but became futile in their thoughts, and their foolish hearts were darkened" (Romans 1:20–21 NKJV).

Are you proclaiming the goodness of God to this generation?

Something that is Common

I was thrilled when I saw a red-winged blackbird in Ohio this summer. I grew up hearing their wonderful sound of the marsh. Spotting their bright red wings on their glowing black body amongst reeds was a common sight for me in New York state, Pennsylvania, and Canada.

Having moved to North Carolina, I had not seen one in ten years. I had forgotten how common they were.

Have you been around someone who "swears like a sailor" and it is common language for you to hear? Or have you been entertained by a favorite show and found yourself numb to the vulgar language? You repeatedly hear swear words and God's name taken in vain. Blasphemy quashes our discernment to be sensitive to God's will and His ways.

My husband used to say, "If you are working on something and curse, asking God to damn it, then how will you fix it if you have just asked God to damn it?" We are to let no unwholesome talk come out of our mouths.

We are to have "sound speech that cannot be condemned, that one who is an opponent may be ashamed, having nothing evil to say of you" (Titus 2:8 NKJV). The scriptures teach us to show integrity, reverence, and incorruptibility.

But we say, "I hear it in the movies and TV shows quite often." Yes, we are foolishly serving our lusts and pleasures, living in malice against God. He asks that we be renewed by "the washing of water by the word" (Ephesians 5:26 NKJV) of God.

> A lover of what is good, sober-minded, just, holy, self-controlled."
>
> TITUS 1:8 (NKJV)

There is an old saying, "Garbage in, garbage out." What are we feeding our spirits?

Hearing God's Voice

It is important to spend time in prayer every day. Not just because it is a good habit, but because God is waiting to meet with us. If He were coming for breakfast what would you do to prepare?

Part of our prayer time is discussion; we talk and He listens. The other part of discussion is our listening, so quiet yourself long enough to listen. Sometimes God reminds us of various things, like someone's birthday or anniversary, some specific person or event that we need to take before the Lord in prayer. He may be speaking to us in conviction over a passage we have read in the Bible. He is also in the process of renewing our mind when we listen to Him.

Do you question if you are really hearing God, or if these are just your own thoughts? Usually He drops something in your spirit that you would not have thought of such as a word, a memory, or a direction to take. Once He told me "That person has integrity." I was young enough, such that I did not know what that word meant so I had to look up the word in the dictionary in order to find its meaning. I knew God spoke to me about that person and event, because I was questioning their motive. I was relieved to know they had integrity.

> For it is God who works in you both to will and to do for *His* good pleasure.
>
> PHILIPPIANS 2:13 (NKJV)

He is working in us. Are we listening? He desires to do His good pleasure. He is doing both: working and willing. Are we tuned into His direction for our lives?

The Mystery of Grace Revealed

When I was eighteen years old, I told my mother that Easter did not hold meaning for me. Yes, it was a beautiful time of the year with flowers blooming after a cold, long New York state winter. She told me the spiritual aspect of Easter would come as a revelation to me if I asked God.

It was that spring when I received Jesus Christ as my Savior. I became "born again."

Jesus answered and said to him, "Most assuredly I say to you, unless one is born again, he cannot see the kingdom of God."

Nicodemus said to Him, "How can a man be born when he is old? Can he enter a second time into his mother's womb and be born?"

Jesus answered, "Most assuredly, I say to you, unless one is born of water and the Spirit, he cannot enter into the kingdom of God. That which is born of flesh is flesh, and that which is born of the Spirit is spirit."

JOHN 3:3–6 (NKJV)

This grace is undeserved favor. I did not deserve eternal life with God in heaven, but deserved death and hell because of my sinful nature. My sin separated me from a Holy God. I was going to die and pay for my sin in hell.

Instead, Jesus paid the price for my sin by dying a painful death on the wooden cross. I became born again. It did come as a revelation to me. In Ephesians 3:2–4 (NKJV) Paul talks about the dispensation of the grace of God … that by a revelation He made known to me the mystery in Christ.

It is a mystery revealed by God to us by His Holy Spirit. It is eternal life spent with God the Father, Jesus Christ the anointed one, and the Holy Spirit. You can have it starting today as I did.

It is a living, breathing relationship with God through Jesus Christ. We have to confess our sin and seek forgiveness through Jesus Christ and His work on the cross. He then cleanses us from all unrighteousness. We can come boldly to the throne of grace.

> In whom we have boldness and access with confidence through faith in Him.
>
> EPHESIANS 3:12 (NKJV)

What kind of relationship do you have with Him? Do you have confidence that you have eternal life? Ask Him to come into your heart today.

Rest

Six days you shall work, but on the seventh day you shall rest; in plowing time and in harvest you shall rest.

EXODUS 34:21 (NKJV)

This is a commandment from the Lord. In fact it is one of the Ten Commandments. It is important that we rest our bodies and rest from our schedules. In America, we are driven by our schedules and noise. Our minds are occupied by our phones and laptops. We watch the clock to see how much we can accomplish. Yet God commands that we take off one day a week to rest. Our son recently traveled to Portugal where they take a siesta every afternoon between three and five o'clock to rest. The shops are closed for business and open again at 5:00 p.m. This command is for our good and not to be followed by the letter of the law, but for our benefit.

We are not only to rest our bodies, but rest in the Lord. Think of a warm bath on a cold winter day, or a comforting blanket as we rest on the couch. This is the kind of rest we can find in God's presence as He calms and soothes us with His presence and promises.

Menuchah means a calm resting place, a place of stillness and peace. We receive consolation and repose from Him in our spirit. Menuchah is derived from the verb Nuach, which is to soothe and settle down. Sometimes we need to settle down in our spirit just like we send our kids to their rooms after bad behavior. We want peace in the house and they need to settle down.

> And He said, "My presence will go *with you*, and I will give you rest.
>
> EXODUS 33:14 (NKJV)

> To whom He said, "This *is* the rest *with which*
> you may cause the weary to rest,"
> And "This *is* the refreshing";
> Yet they would not hear.
>
> ISAIAH 28:12 (NKJV)

Take the time to rest and stop pushing yourself. God desires that we rest in Him.

Spiritual Blessings

Blessed *be* the God and Father of our Lord Jesus Christ, who has blessed us with every spiritual blessing in the heavenly *places* in Christ, just as He chose us in Him before the foundation of the world, that we should be holy and without blame before Him in love.

EPHESIANS 1:3–4 (NKJV)

Let's consider these two verses. It starts out by praising God the Father, Jesus, and His Father's Father blessing us. We bless Him and in return He blesses us with spiritual blessings in heavenly places. We cannot see these blessings until we look through our spiritual eyes. These resources available to us are the gifts of the Holy Spirit.

> Love, joy, peace, longsuffering, kindness, goodness, faithfulness, gentleness, self-control. Against such there is no law.
>
> GALATIANS 5:22—23 (NKJV)

"Against such there is no law." Have you heard the expression "there is no speed limit"?

We can receive and own these when we are in a relationship with God, the Father, through Jesus Christ, and His work on the cross through the power of the Holy Spirit.

He chose us and thought of us before the foundation of the earth. Think of that!

He wants us to be holy and without blame before Him in love. He desires to gift us with the fruit of the spirit mentioned above; not that we can be patient all the time or long suffering on our own. He gives us His spirit to carry out these characteristics when we are in a relationship with Him. He provided His son to die for our sins so we can be blameless before Him. Praise be to our Holy God.

Selfishness

But know this, that in the last days perilous times will come: For men will be lovers of themselves, lovers of money, boasters, proud, blasphemes, disobedient to parents, unthankful, unholy, unloving, unforgiving, slanderers without self-control, brutal, despisers of good, traitors, headstrong, haughty, lovers of pleasure rather than lovers of God.

II TIMOTHY 3:1-4 (NKJV)

How often do we talk about the end times? Asking questions of others, "Do you think we are living in the last days or end of times?" My dad, who lived until his nineties, felt he was living in the end of times. He passed away ten years ago. End of time scriptures refers to birth pangs. The pangs of contractions during childbirth come with more frequency before giving birth. According to scripture, this means the frequency of selfishness appears more often in our culture.

My dad experienced the Great Depression, World War I and World War II, the Korean War, and the Vietnam War. He saw the selfish characteristics of man bent toward evil increase towards the end of his ninety-six years.

We believe it was Solomon who wrote in Ecclesiastes "that which has been *is* what will be, that which *is* done is what will be done, and *there is* nothing new under the sun" (Ecclesiastes 1:9 NKJV).

We have witnessed the breakdown of our culture in selfish acts of abortion, pornography, fornication, adultery, homosexuality, homosexual attraction, and now same-sex marriage. Blasphemy against God on TV and in the movies, reckless living, lying, and cheating are everywhere. None of it is new under heaven, but yes, with new blatant frequency and little conviction, we are experiencing birth pangs.

We must not become numb to these offenses because they offend God. We must accept to live in His love and not our own self love.

> My God shall supply all your needs according to his riches in glory by Christ Jesus.
>
> PHILIPPIANS 4:19 (NKJV)

The flood

You heard it said that in the last days it will be just as in the time of Noah that the end will come.

> And as it was in the days of Noah, so it will be also in the days of the Son of Man: They ate, they drank, they married wives, they were given in marriage, until the day that Noah entered the ark, and the flood came and destroyed them all.
>
> LUKE 17:26 (NKJV)

We know that God destroyed the earth by a worldwide flood. He has promised not to destroy it again by a flood.

God is saying "even so it will be in the day when the Son of Man is revealed" (Luke 17:30 NKJV). God is talking about Jesus coming back for the second time. Jesus will come back to judge the earth and its inhabitants and then restore the earth to its original flawless state.

So what is different about the times of Noah and today? We are still eating and drinking and getting married. We have to look back to the time of Noah when people were living recklessly.

> Then the LORD saw that the wickedness of man *was* great in the earth and *that* every intent of the thoughts of his heart *was* only evil continually. And the LORD was sorry that He had made man on the earth, and He was grieved in His heart.
>
> GENESIS 6:5–6 (NKJV)

I do believe God is very grieved today to see how His creation is living. How about you? Are you grieving His heart by the way you are living? Ask God to reveal what grieves His heart today. He is a God of grace and forgiveness. Repent, ask for His forgiveness, and be set free to live the life He intended for you.

Woody Woodpecker

My husband and I had a dead widow-maker tree branch removed from an oak tree over our driveway. The branch was cut up into two-foot sections and dropped to the ground with many thuds that shook the ground and the whole house. This happened at 6 a.m. in the morning as the tree trimmers start early in the summertime.

Momma, a red-bellied woodpecker, flew off in dismay over losing her home and her babies. One baby lie on the ground after falling from the tree branch thirty feet above to the ground. It was, by some miracle, still alive. My husband

and I waited an hour and a half, but Momma did not return. My husband suggested I place the baby bird in an occupied wren's nest under our deck.

By late afternoon the baby woodpecker had fallen out of the nest, or perhaps it had been removed by the existing mother wren. We placed him back in the nest only to find him on the pavement in the morning. His body was cold and my first thought was he was dead. I went to take him to the woods only to find him chirping and stretching his pink wings. He had no peach fuzz and no feathers. He had lost body weight from the day before. I quickly placed him in warm water to bring his body temperature up and, to my surprise, he drank the warm water. He was a survivor.

We brought him inside and placed him in a basket with a heating pad underneath to keep his body temperature at ninety-eight to ninety-nine degrees. I placed him near the kitchen sink for easy access to feed him. We started a feeding regimen of dried mealworms soaked in diluted coconut water every hour during the day. We fed him with tweezers much like his mom's beak. He was appropriately named Woody. He constantly sang and became louder at meal time. He appeared very happy.

My husband found live mealworms in the woods and we gave them to Woody. They were juicy and plump and very difficult for me to look at and serve. However, I felt privileged to care for such a wonderful creation of God, a wild red-bellied woodpecker.

By the end of the ninety-degree day, the mealworms were getting slimy and had a stench. At this point, I could not stand the smell or their appearance. Woody took one meal worm in his beak and spun his neck around and flung that worm out of his mouth. I knew at this point the mealworms had gone bad. We were all done with the live mealworms. The sight and stench of the worms stayed with me into that evening. The Lord reminded me of the church in Laodicea.

Revelations 3:16 (NKJV) says the same about the church at Laodicea, "So then, because you are lukewarm, and neither cold nor hot, I will vomit you out of My mouth." In other words, the church was nauseating to our Most High God in thought, taste, and feel. They were lukewarm and not serving God nor sold out to Him. God help us that we remain steadfast in our fellowship and relationship with God.

Trees of Righteousness

Did you know that we are to be compared to a strong mature oak tree? A planting of the Lord?

> That they may be called trees of righteousness,
> The planting of the LORD, that He may be glorified.
>
> ISAIAH 61:3 (NKJV)

Yes, He has planted us and gave us life. Our lives are to grow mature for His glory. I can just see your strong trunk and branches with leaves displayed for His Glory. Do our lives display the glory of God?

Did you know that the oak tree has a very deep root

system that goes down deep into the earth? It is unlike the pine tree that can topple in a strong gust of wind because its roots are shallow.

Our roots are to be grounded in His love. Ephesians tells us "that Christ may dwell in your hearts though faith; that you, being rooted and grounded in love, may be able to comprehend with all the saints what *is* the width and length and depth and height—to know this love of Christ which passes knowledge; that you may be filled with the fullness of God" (Ephesians 3:17–19 NKJV).

Is your root system grounded in His love? This is amazing that He holds us steady in the strong winds of life. He loves us and holds us in His love.

A Psalm tells us "He shall be like a tree planted by the rivers of water, that brings forth its fruit in its season, whose leaf also shall not wither; and whatever he does shall prosper" (Psalm 1:3 NKJV). Are we watered by the word of God, bringing forth fruits of righteousness? The scriptures tie it all together so beautifully.

The Weight of Our Lives

Recently I experienced the tedious process of watching our building contractor place sliding glass doors in our new home. The doors weighed 400 lbs. and had to be lifted up ten feet to be placed in the wall of our sunroom. Two sets of doors had been delivered damaged and required replacement after they were nearly installed.

This day I watched six workers carefully supporting and lifting the doors while working on ladders as our builder raised the doors while he worked the forklift. The doors were tipped to one side as they were lifted from the ground. I could clearly see they needed to be set in place perfectly in the wall.

I found myself praying for God's grace to see this timely project completed. Might I add these doors were very expensive. Just before the doors were set down and placed forward into the walls, there was a caulk seal that had to be placed all around the door frame to make a watertight seal protecting the windows from the outside weather.

It was so tedious to watch that I prayed and walked away. I said, "Lord you handle this, I cannot watch."

And so it is with our lives. Our lives are precious in His sight—directed, timed, balanced, ordered, secured, and sealed. Just as the doors were directed to the correct level, ten feet off the ground, there were six installers lifting and guiding them on ladders to set them in place. They were very heavy and difficult to balance with the forklift. If those doors dropped off the forklift, they would have been useless. As I had mentioned, two sets of sliding glass doors had to be returned because they had been damaged in the delivery process because they were set on their side resulting in the bending of their frame.

As the scriptures says, "He cuts our channels in the rocks, and his eye sees every precious thing" (Job 28:10 NKJV).

The steps of a *good* man are ordered by the LORD,
And He delights in his way.

PSALM 37:23 (NKJV)

Many, O Lord my God, *are* Your wonderful works,
Which You have done,
And Your thoughts toward us
Cannot be recounted to You in order:
If I would declare and speak of *them*,
They are more than can be numbered.

PSALM 40:5 (NKJV)

How much more are our lives ordered of God if we allow Him to direct us? Just as the doors were caulked and sealed, so are our lives.

In Him you also *trusted*, after you heard the word of truth, the gospel of your salvation; in whom also, having believed, you were sealed with the Holy Spirit of promise.

EPHESIANS 1:13 (NKJV)

The Lion and the Donkey

One day a man of God was instructed by God not to go into a person's dwelling. He was not to eat the bread or drink the water of that place. (I Kings 13:16 NKJV) This other man who claimed to be a prophet of God lied to the man of God and told him "I too *am* a prophet as you *are*, and an angel spoke to me by the word of the LORD saying, 'Bring him back with you to your house, that we may eat bread and drink water'" (I Kings 13:18 NKJV).

The man of God did exactly what God had warned him not to do. He ate and drank at the second prophet's house. How many times have we believed someone who lied? Or someone gave us a warning of advice that we did not take seriously?

Later that day the first prophet who heard the warning from God saddled his donkey and rode away. A lion met him on the road and killed him.

> And his corpse was thrown on the road, and the donkey stood by it. The lion also stood by the corpse.
>
> I KINGS 13:24 (NKJV)

Isn't it interesting that the lion who killed the man of God did not eat him or eat the donkey? God had left evidence of the prophet's death.

Where was God's justice? Why didn't the man who lied get killed?

The man of God who was a prophet was disobedient to his Heavenly Father. How careful we must be to discern the Lord's voice. We must not be swayed or listen to the voice of deception.

Strength in Weakness

And He said to me, "My strength is sufficient for you, for My strength is made perfect in weakness." Therefore most gladly I will rather boast in my infirmities, that the power of Christ may rest upon me.

II CORINTHIANS 12:9 (NKJV)

Jesus is speaking the first part of this verse and Paul writes the second part.

Jesus is saying His grace is sufficient for us and His strength made perfect in our weakness. Paul would boast in his infirmities that the power of Christ would rest on him.

God revealed this verse to me while I laid in a hospital bed after back surgery. I kept asking Him, "How is this going to work? How are you going to do just that? How will you, God, be my strength when I am so weak from surgery?"

My husband took care of me that first week at home after surgery, providing meals, bathing, and dressing me. I had no idea I would be so weak and not be able to take care of myself.

He went out of town the second week that I was home from the hospital. Our son was living with us at the time, but he worked out of town and was gone twelve hours a day due to his commute. There was no one at home to help me. If I prepared a meal for myself, by the time I had finished, I was too exhausted to eat it.

I was feeling like I was up a creek with no boat or paddle. How was I to take care of myself, let alone fix a meal?

The Lord said to me, "Every day ask for your needs in prayer and list them." This meant He wanted me to ask Him and ask others to help me. This meant I had to ask someone to clean the bathroom and the kitty litter, yuk! So every day I thought of my needs and prayed to God that he would send someone.

Each day I petitioned God for my needs. In humility, I let others know of my needs. God did provide through human hands. It was the body of Christ that represented His strength as they ministered to my needs. The people who helped me were an extension of Christ's body.

His grace is sufficient and His strength is made perfect in weakness. He gets the glory!!!

Rejoicing in Labor

Here is what I have seen: *It is* good and fitting *for one* to eat and drink, and to enjoy the good of all his labor in which he toils under the sun all the days of his life which God gives him; for it *is* his heritage. As for every man to whom God has given riches and wealth, and given him power to eat of it, to receive his heritage and rejoice in his labor—this is a gift of God.

ECCLESIASTES 5:18–19 (NKJV)

It is a gift from God that we are able to work. He has given us the health, skills, and the value of a hard-earned dollar. We are to rejoice in our labor and be able to eat, drink, and live comfortably. Enjoying life is a heritage from the Lord.

Is work difficult at times? Yes! You may have worked for a difficult boss who is hard to please. Someone who feels you never measure up or do enough. Then do your work as unto the Lord. He, the Lord, is the ultimate authority on how well you have performed. Ask God if He is pleased with your labor. Then enjoy the fruit of your labor.

I knew someone who sacrificed and said they were not taking a salary at all for their family business. They had no income and wondered why they were struggling. My reply was that it is not scriptural principle. God expects us to be paid for our labor.

> The laborer *is* worthy of his wages.
>
> I TIMOTHY 5:18 (NKJV)

I have known of preachers who have taken royalties from books they have written and not taken a salary from their ministries. Their royalties have provided enough income for them to support their families. God will supply all our needs if we live by His principles. We can enjoy and rejoice in our labor.

Red Clay

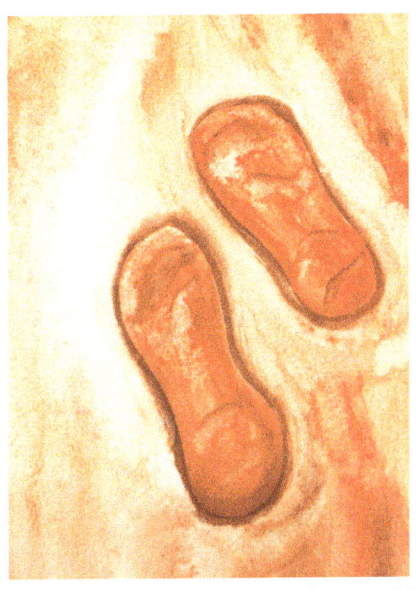

We recently moved into our new house. My husband requested that we have a shower in the garage for the dogs. It has been wonderful to clean up the dogs' paws in the shower before they enter the house. You see, we live in North Carolina where the soil contains red clay. Whenever I clean off their paws with the warm water in the shower, I watch the red clay and dirt go down the drain with full satisfaction.

Isn't it amazing that my sin is washed away when I confess it to the Lord? The visual for me is to watch the red clay go right down the drain.

"Come now, and let us reason together,"
Says the LORD
"Though your sins are like scarlet,
they shall be as white as snow;
Though they are red like crimson,
They shall be as wool."

ISAIAH 1:18 (NKJV)

It is though the sacrificial blood of Jesus that we have been cleansed of our sin.

But God demonstrates His own love towards us, in that while we were still sinners, Christ died for us.

ROMANS 5:8 (NKJV)

For the wages of sin *is* death, but the gift of God *is* eternal life in Christ Jesus our Lord.

ROMANS 6:23 (NKJV)

Repay no one evil for evil. Have regard for good things in the sight of all men.

ROMANS 12:17 (NKJV)

The discretion of a man makes him slow to anger,
And his glory *is* to overlook a transgression.

PROVERBS 19:11 (NKJV)

Before I enter God's presence in prayer, I am reminded of my own heart and sinful nature. Have I forgiven that someone? Have I had a bad attitude? Have I been selfish with my time? Am I neglecting someone else's needs? I am not worthy to enter into His presence until I have examined my own paws to see if they are dirty. I am so grateful for His mercy and grace to wash my clay-stained sins away.

Our Anguish and Our Hope

I was walking in the woods in the spring of the year and noticed the new growth on the forest floor. Boston ferns were just beginning to unfold and small white flowers had bloomed on the side of the creek bed. There were wild strawberry plants and wild purple violets that had budded. Up towards the sky, buds were forming on the trees and the pink cherry trees were awakened from their slumber. By contrast, I noticed several downed, dead, rotting trees that had been in a state of decay for years.

Through the LORD's mercies we are not consumed,

Because His compassions fail not.

They are new every morning.

Great *is* your faithfulness.

LAMENTATIONS 3:22–23 (NKJV)

Just as we experience spring every year, every year we are guaranteed spring. So are God's mercies a guarantee.

The LORD *is* good to those who wait for Him.

LAMENTATIONS 3:25 (NKJV)

For the Lord will not cast off forever.

Though He causes grief,

Yet He will show compassion

According to the multitude of His mercies.

For he does not afflict willingly,

Nor grieve the children of men.

LAMENTATIONS 3:31-33 (NKJV)

You may relate to the downed trees in the woods that seem oh so dreary. You may have come though a difficult time; difficulty because of your own decisions and failures. Or those difficult times may have been brought on by the decisions of others.

Upon closer inspection, you can see new life in the woods as promised by the word of God. His mercies are new every morning. His compassion will not fail. You do not have to be afraid of tomorrow. Your situation does not have to repeat itself.

> The LORD *is* good to those who wait for Him,
> To the soul *who* seeks Him.
>
> LAMENTATIONS 3:25 (NKJV)

Mistaken Identity

Transgender, homosexual, bisexual, same-sex marriage, shacking up, fake news. These are all current popular terms. Guess what? God calls these sin. They are not what God created us to be. We are His image barriers.

Fake news is simply lies. Shacking up is fornication. Homosexual, transgender, bisexual are all an abomination to the Lord.

God created us as male and female. At birth we were specifically created with a set of male or female chromosomes. We never lose them to our drying day. God has a purpose for His creation to be male and female so that we may be fruitful and multiply.

Gender confusion is part of Satan's plan. He is the author of confusion and lies. He comes to kill, steal, and destroy.

Couples today think nothing of shacking up. This goes against God's design for a perfect union between male and female. God asks for a lifetime covenant between a man and a woman before Him. This marriage forms one family unit and leads to procreation of offspring. This covenant relationship is the bedrock of society and brings security to the wife and children.

So how are we to handle these sins that surround us that are so prevalent today?

First we love the person and not their sinful behavior. We do not have to accept these behaviors as the norm; according to the word of God they are still called sin. "There but for the grace of God, go I." This world needs more love and not judgment. We are to teach these behaviors as contrary to God's plan for mankind. God has something so much better for us.

> So God created man in His *own* image; in the image of God He created him; male and female He created them.
>
> GENESIS 1:27 (NKJV)

> Therefore a man shall leave his father and mother and be joined to his wife, and they shall become one flesh.
>
> GENESIS 2:24 (NKJV)

For God is not *the author* of confusion but of peace, as in all the churches of the saints.

            I CORINTHIANS 14:33 (NKJV)

The thief does not come except to steal, and to kill and to destroy. I have come that they may have life, and that they may have *it* more abundantly.

                JOHN 10:10 (NKJV)

God's Temple

The Israelites worshipped the Lord in a tent called a tabernacle while moving about in the wilderness. David longed to build a permanent building: a temple to replace the tabernacle.

Solomon, the son of David built the temple that David longed to build for the LORD (I Kings 5:5).

Solomon built a magnificent temple. When he finished the temple "Solomon brought in the things which his father David had dedicated: the silver and gold and the furnishings. He put them in the treasuries of the house of the LORD" (I Kings 7:51 NKJV).

Then Solomon asked, "But will God indeed dwell on the earth? Behold, heaven and the heaven of heavens cannot contain You. How much less this temple which I have built!" (I Kings 8:27 NKJV).

Under the new covenant, God refers to us as His Temple.

> Do you not know that you are the temple of God and *that* the Spirit of God dwells in you?
>
> I CORINTHIANS 3:16 (NKJV)

So the question is: How is your temple? It involves our mind, soul, spirit, and physical body.

Is it kept clean and in order for the Lord to dwell there?

Gender Identity Confusion

So God created man in His *own* image; in the image of God He created him; male and female He created them.

GENESIS 1:27 (NKJV)

Therefore a man shall leave his father and mother and be joined to his wife, and they shall become one flesh.

GENESIS 2:24 (NKJV)

And he answered and said to them, "Have you not read that He who made *them* at the beginning 'made them male and female.'"

MATTHEW 19:4 (NKJV)

So then, they are no longer two but one flesh. Therefore what God has joined together let not man separate.

MATTHEW 19:6 (NKJV)

We hear a lot in the media and social networking about gender identity. Conservative Christians are calling this gender confusion. No wonder God in His word speaks to the issue of gender. From the beginning, he created us as male and female. As in the act of creation, children have been born for centuries as male and female.

Your eyes saw my substance, being yet unformed.
And in Your book they all were written,
The days fashioned for me,
When *as yet there were* none of them.

PSALM 139:16 (NKJV)

In His wisdom He created us and designed us with DNA/chromosome structure before we were even conceived in our mother's womb. He planned for our sex long before we were born.

Currently, children have been taken away from their

parents by the state because the child chooses to be of a different sex. Some parents have desired to have a child of the opposite sex and dressed them as such. Some have gone as far as hormone replacement therapy at puberty, which cannot be reversed. This is not at all God's design for our children. He created us as male and female. Rejoice in the way God made you.

Elijah and the Widow

During a drought, God had instructed Elijah the prophet to go to Zarephath. There he was to find a widow that God had commanded to provide food for Elijah.

The widow had a handful of flour in a bin and a little oil in a jar. She planned to make bread, feed her son, and then die. Elijah asked that she make him some first. "Elijah said to her 'Do not fear; go *and* do as you have said, but make me a small cake from it first, and bring *it* to me; and afterward make some for yourself and your son'" (I Kings 17:13 NKJV).

This was a huge sacrifice for the widow because this was all she had left to eat. Elijah told her not to fear, for God would provide for her and her son. Her oil would not run dry, nor her flour run out until the Lord sent rain upon the earth.

Sometimes our finances run thin and God asks that we give sacrificially to Him in a tithe or to give to another person in need. Oh yes, it is sacrifice and scary, however, God is faithful to provide when we are obedient and put Him first.

> She went away and did according to the word of Elijah; and she and he and her household ate for *many* days.
>
> I KINGS 17:15 (NKJV)

> And my God shall supply all your need according to His riches in glory by Christ Jesus. Now to our God and Father *be* glory forever and ever. Amen.
>
> PHILIPPIANS 4:19–20 (NKJV)

Be obedient to God and trust Him with your finances. He wants to provide for you.

Higher Ground

Scripturally speaking a **_covenant_** is an agreement between man and God. Marriage in the eyes of God is a covenant. We have the Old Testament, which is the Old Covenant, and then the New Testament, which is the New Covenant. There are many covenants in the scriptures between man and God. The rainbow is one we are all familiar with. God promised not to flood the earth again with the display of the rainbow.

We think today in terms of a **_contract_** as a legal document. We have contracts for cars we buy or lease for three to five years. Home mortgages for fifteen to twenty years. A contract can be ended and usually has terms of agreement to end. It usually involves money; it does not involve God.

In a contract you may see marriage as mutually beneficial. You can even make a prenuptial agreement where you make no lasting commitment in your marriage, but may agree to end the marriage if you think it is not working out. There is no lifetime commitment to your spouse or God.

A covenant should also be mutually agreed upon and beneficial to both parties, however, there may come a time with our vows when there is "sickness or health, better or worse." No matter what—loss of a job, loss of a loved one, physical or emotional storms. We will experience the valleys. With a covenant you are committed to the marriage for the long run; which is very comforting to your spouse and creates a secure environment. The covenant agreement looks to give and not to get. You are to focus on your spouse's needs and this brings about mutual fulfillment. We are to stay focused on the positive qualities of our spouse and remind them often of these good qualities. No one is perfect. We all have weaknesses, so we offer forgiveness. Each spouse must give one hundred percent to the relationship. This is a covenant marriage.

"But this is the Covenant I will make with the house of Israel after those days says the Lord. 'I will put my law in their minds, and write it on their hearts; and I will be their God and they shall be my people.' (Jeremiah 31:33 NKJV) Also see Hebrew 8:10 and Hebrews 10:16–17.

Where the Rubber Meets the Road

In marriage we can love the person, but hate their behavior. Yes, it does come to this sometimes. We experience behaviors we do not like in our spouse. We cannot change their behavior, but we can let them know it bothers us. If you love your spouse, you will work to change the undesirable behaviors.

Love is confusing as we hurt the people we love the most. Love is an action word. We can say, "I do not love you any more" all because we are hurting. It is the behavior you hate, but the person you love. So you choose to love as a verb, not an emotion. I love you, but do not trust you. Trust has to be earned.

I forgive you, but I do not trust you yet. Please forgive me, I do love you and I will work to change those undesirable behaviors. Forgiveness is a decision and not an emotion. We choose to forgive and with God's help and His power we can forgive just as God has forgiven us. When we choose to forgive and it is a decision to forgive, we may not feel like it. As we begin the process of forgiveness, the emotion will follow where we feel like forgiving.

Couples divorce today because of spiritual differences, unfaithfulness, and physical and emotional abuse. Today's couples divorce for selfish reasons and unmet expectations that have not been clearly communicated. There are exceptions for divorce and it is needed to bring about peace to the wounded spouse.

What patterns of behaviors does your spouse find irritating in you? What behaviors do they just love? Ask them.

Conviction vs. Condemnation

Do you find yourself living with guilt even when you asked for forgiveness? We can live under the weight of condemnation and not be free to enjoy God's presence. Some carry guilt for years from experiences such as having had an abortion and never having experienced God's forgiveness. Why is that? There may be several reasons. Have you forgiven others of their offenses against you?

> For if you forgive men their trespasses, your Heavenly Father will also forgive you. But if you do not forgive men

their trespasses, neither will your Father forgive your trespasses.

MATHEW 6:14—15 (NKJV)

We may live under condemnation because we have not forgiven ourselves. Jesus paid the price for our sins and we must acknowledge that his death and crucifixion was enough.

If we confess our sins, He is faithful and just to forgive us *our* sins and to cleanse us from all unrighteousness.

1 JOHN 1:9 (NKJV)

As far as the east is from the west,
So far has He removed our transgressions from us.

PSALMS 103:12 (NKJV)

He remembers them no more than we do remember our sins, and this serves to remind us to not repeat them.

Condemnation is different than conviction. Condemnation comes from self and others, while conviction comes from God. Some people will try to make us feel guilty like we have done something wrong and our best is not good enough. This is condemnation. Those words and thoughts are demonic and from Satan. He is the father of lies. That guilt is not from God. In fact, ask God how you did in that particular situation. Were you honest and did you do your best? Was God pleased?

Conviction is of the Holy Spirit. We know it in our spirit that God is convicting us. We ask for forgiveness. We are genuine in our repentance and do a 180 to stop that behavior. With true repentance and change we do not live with guilt. God has wiped the slate clean and we live with God's mercy and grace.

> In Him we have redemption through His blood, the forgiveness of sins, according to the riches of His grace.
>
> EPHESIANS 1:7 (NKJV)

With conviction of the Holy Spirit, we confess and feel refreshed. His conviction draws us closer to God.

Coming to the End of Ourselves

Jonah began to enter the city on the first day's walk. Then he cried out and said, "Yet forty days, and Nineveh shall be overthrown!"

JONAH 3:4 (NKJV)

Nineveh was opposite the city of Mosul in modern Iraq.

Jonah did not want to go to Nineveh to deliver God's message of repentance. Instead Jonah traveled in the opposite direction to get away from God's call on his life to speak to the city of Nineveh.

Jonah had been at sea in a storm due to his disobedience to the will of God. He was thrown overboard and swallowed by a great fish. You may remember the children's Bible story of Jonah and the great fish?

After three days, Jonah repented before God and the great fish vomited Jonah onto dry ground. Jonah did go and preach repentance to the city of Nineveh. He was probably exhausted from his experience in the great fish and traveling in such a large city proclaiming the word of the Lord. (Nineveh was sixty miles in circumference.)

Jonah speaks, "Therefore now, O Lord, please take my life from me, for *it is* better for me to die than to live!" (Jonah 4:3 NKJV). "Then the Lord said, '*Is it* right for you to be angry?'" (Jonah 4:4 NKJV).

Jonah was not happy that God in His mercy had spared the city of Nineveh. Jonah had come to the end of himself. He was depressed, angry, and exhausted. God did come and minister to his spiritual and physical needs through rest.

Have you ever noticed how life seems worse when you are exhausted? Situations seem worse than they are at night and somehow seem much less troublesome in the morning. Allow God to minister to you both physically and spiritually when you are exhausted. Slow down and take the time you need to rest. Pray and ask God what it is He wants to show you.

Chocolate Chip Cookies

The words of a talebearer are like tasty trifles.
And they go down into the inmost body.

PROVERBS 18:8 (NKJV)

Have you ever experienced chocolate chip cookies hot out of the oven? The chocolate chip cookies melt in your mouth. Or have you eaten chocolate chips right out of the bag before baking? It can be hard to stop eating them to leave enough for baking your recipe. Chocolate chip cookies go down easily—and so do rumors.

The first *one* to plead his cause *seems* right,
Until his neighbor comes and examines him.

PROVERBS 18:17 (NKJV)

We must ask ourselves: What is the truth in every situation? What is the other side of the story? Is this true or is this a rumor? It is easy to get sucked into an elaborate story that sounds believable and fits the situation perfectly. Ask yourself, is there another side to the story? I need to get the facts. There is great danger in spreading false rumors about people and situations.

Jesus said "I am the way the truth and the light."

Get all the advice and instruction you can, so you will be wise the rest of your life.

PROVERBS 19:20 (NLT)

Buoys in the Water

On our recent trip to Maine we experienced thick fog that covered the waters and coast of Bass Harbor. The blanket of fog hiding the sun made for cool days and brisk nights. When we arrived, we could not see past the edge of the property that edged the water thirty feet in front of us.

As one day passed, the fog began to recede back out of the harbor. We could now see the separation of land and water on the edge of the property. By day three, we could see half of the harbor unfold through the fog. As the fog receded, we noticed several buoys in the water. The lobster fisherman had placed their traps down under the water and marked them by buoys on top of the water. Every lobster fisherman could identify their own trap by the painted markings on their buoys.

We saw at least fifty and then a hundred buoys in the water. When the sun broke through and the weather warmed to eighty degrees, we noticed not one hundred but a thousand buoys and lobster traps in the bay much to our surprise, as we did not realize the extent of the lobster traps in Bass Harbor Bay.

Like the lobster fishermen, we too have placed our prayers before the throne of God. Each is individually packaged with our name attached. Each trap may contain a few lobsters or more but it is not until the fog rolls away and the trap is brought to the surface that the fisherman can cash in his catch.

So it is with our prayers.

> Seek first the kingdom of God and His righteousness, and all these things shall be added to you.
>
> MATTHEW 6:33 (NKJV)

If we put God first and offer our prayer requests to Him, we do not always see our prayers answered in a timely manner.

> Now He who searches the hearts knows what the mind of the Spirit *is*, because He makes intercession for the saints according to *the will of* God.
>
> ROMANS 8:27 (NKJV)

So we know that Jesus sits at the right-hand of God, the Father, making intercession for us. Just like the fog, the triune God is working under a veil behind the scenes on our behalf. If He does not seem to be answering our prayers, He may be working on some right now that we are not aware of, off in the distance working out His plans for us.

There are times when the fishing boats run over the buoys and the lines are cut, breaking free from the lobster traps. The picture depicts the buoys that broke free from the traps and were brought to shore by the tide. The buoys were collected and placed on the back of the well house. How many times have we stopped seeking God's will and stopped praying and taken matters into our own hands? Like the lobster catch that is still on the bottom of the ocean, we have missed out on what God has for us. Similarly, we leave God and our prayer line.

Once we cut the line to the lobster trap, it is similar to having cut our line to God. We, like the buoys, drift to shore never fulfilling our purpose. Leaving our treasure behind.

> Now to Him who is able to do exceedingly abundantly above all that we ask or think, according to the power that works in us.
>
> EPHESIANS 3:20 (NKJV)

Appointed Time

He appointed the moon for seasons;

The sun knows it's going down.

You make darkness and it is night.

In which all the beasts of the forest creep about.

The young lions roar after their prey,

And seek their food from God.

When the sun rises, they gather together

And lie down in their dens.

Man goes out to his work.

And to his labor until evening.

O LORD, how manifold are Your works!

In wisdom you have made them all.

The earth is full of Your possessions.

PSALM 104:19-24 (NKJV)

We all need routine. While showing our house to sell, we moved items such as garbage cans, Kleenex boxes, towels, and pillows. I stopped counting the times I reached for a towel to find it not there, but rather a new fluffy towel not to be used. It was placed strategically only for staging the house. The same with the garbage can. I would subconsciously walk by where we had kept the garbage can with something in my hand to throw away only to find it had been moved.

We are creatures of habit and routine. God created us this way. Babies need schedules, toddlers need routine. We find comfort to know where things can be found and to have starting and ending times.

Aren't you glad for the sun and the moon, darkness for night, light for day. We know our daily routine. Stop and thank the Lord for the order of life.

A Worldview versus a Biblical View

As I am writing this, it has been a year of political battles dividing Christians in the body of Christ and labeling Christians as bigots in the world's eyes. We all experience racial, economic, political, social, and gender differences. Satan has chosen these to divide us. Paul writes "There is neither Jew or Greek, there is neither slave or free, there is neither male nor female, for you are all one in Christ Jesus" (Galatians 3:28 NKJV).

We are to love everyone equally. We are to love and not attack someone else's view point that they might have posted on Facebook, Twitter, or any other social media platform.

Christians are more conservative than liberals because of the teachings of the Bible that keep social practices in line with a Biblical worldview. Marriage is between a man and a woman versus same-sex marriage (Romans 1:24-27 NKJV). Keep the marriage bed within the boundaries of marriage instead of sleeping together or shacking up (Ephesians 5:1-6, 22-23 NKJV). Carry a baby full-term to deliver instead of aborting the child (Luke 17:3-4 NKJV). Love the soul and spirit of a man or woman and do not judge their appearance by the color of their skin (John 4:9 NKJV). We are to pray for those who persecute us (Luke 17:3-4 NKJV). We are to lovingly proclaim the hope that we have in Jesus Christ, not with judgment but with the same grace God has given us.

Most likely Christians who hold a worldview that differs from the above have not been liberated by Jesus Christ. In others words, they have not been taught the word of God. Most often they need to be discipled and taught, not given opinions, but the correct revealed truth in the word of God.

A Thick Cloud

The Israelites worshipped God in a tent as they traveled though the wilderness. God led them though the wilderness with a cloud by day and a fire by night.

> And it came to pass, when the priests came out of the holy *place*, that the cloud filled the house of the LORD, so that the priests could not continue ministering because of the cloud; for the glory of the LORD filled the house of the LORD.
>
> Then Solomon spoke:
> "The LORD said He would dwell in a dark cloud.
> I surely have built You an exalted house,

And a place for you to dwell in forever."

I KINGS 8:10—13 (NKJV)

God's presence was so strong and thick in the temple it stopped the priests from ministering and carrying out their priestly duties. How often do we get caught up in the ministry and actually neglect to seek God's presence? We can get distracted by works.

Sometimes we need to stop from our labors and enjoy God's presence. Just enjoy spending time with Him in either prayer, reading scripture, or listening to worship music. Not doing works, but enjoying spending time with him.

www.ingramcontent.com/pod-product-compliance
Lightning Source LLC
Chambersburg PA
CBHW062028290426
44108CB00025B/2825